TH ULTIMATE CYCLING QUIZ BOOK

PHILIP CARTER

THE ULTIMATE CYCLING QUIZ BOOK EXPLAINED

From BMX to Cyclo-Cross and Alpe d'Huez to Mont Ventoux, this quiz book comprises 80 quizzes each containing ten questions to test the expertise of even the most ardent cycling fan.

If you know who won the Polka Dot jersey in 2002 or the name of the band that released 'The Pushbike Song' then this is the book for you.

All facts correct up to October 2022.

CONTENTS

QUIZ 1:

ITS ALL ABOUT THE BIKE (1)

1. In what year was the bicycle invented?
2. Who invented the first bicycle?
3. Which bicycle manufacturer has won the most Tours de France?
4. What were the first two mass-produced Mountain Bikes?
5. The manufacturer, Brompton, is traditionally associated with which type of bicycle?
6. In which Tour de France were Tri Bars first used?
7. Which bicycle manufacturer produces the 'Gain' electric bike?
8. In what year was the 'Fizik' brand established?
9. Which manufacturer makes 'Dura Ace' components?
10. Who was the first rider to win a Grand Tour stage using a bicycle equipped with hydraulic disc brakes?

QUIZ 2:

ITS ALL ABOUT THE BIKE (2)

1. Which company produced the 'Spinaci' handlebar extensions?
2. Who invented the first cycle computer?
3. Which company made the aerodynamic 'Espada' bicycle?
4. Fulcrum Wheels is a subsidiary of which company?
5. What brand of bicycle was the winner of the 2020 Tour de France riding?
6. Which company, since 2014, has established a virtual World for cyclists to interact, train and compete in, using stationary 'smart' trainers?
7. Who, in 1992, engineered and developed the World's first ever carbon fibre crank?
8. What are the two types of valve commonly found on modern bicycle inner tubes?
9. Which company launched the Liv sub-brand with products focused exclusively on the female cycling market?
10. Why were Spinergy Rev-X wheels banned by cycling's governing body, the UCI?

QUIZ 3:
THE UCI (1)

1. What does UCI stand for?
2. In what year was the UCI founded?
3. Who was the first President of the UCI?
4. In which town and country would you find the headquarters of the UCI?
5. Who was elected President of the UCI in September 2017?
6. How many countries were originally affiliated to the UCI?
7. What subsidiary bodies were established in 1965 and existed until 1992 when they were reunified and merged back into the UCI?
8. What did the UCI construct, adjacent to its headquarters, in 2004?
9. What new rule resulted in a rider strike at the 1991 Paris-Nice race?
10. Who was the first woman to be appointed as Vice-President of the UCI?

QUIZ 4:
THE UCI (2)

1. In what year was the UCI Road World Cup established?
2. In 2005, what now defunct series replaced the UCI Road World Cup?
3. Which rider had his riding position banned by the UCI, only finding out one hour before he began the 1994 World Championship pursuit in Italy?
4. In 2020, how many national federations were represented by the UCI?
5. To combat doping in the sport the UCI collaborates with which global entity?
6. What is the name of the Irishman who was UCI President between 2005 and 2013?
7. Can you name the former Team HTC-Colombia owner who became Chairman of the Board of USA in 2014?
8. What has the UCI created to promote cities and regions that invest in cycling?
9. Why did the UCI sue Floyd Landis in 2011?
10. Name the five continental confederations.

QUIZ 5:
CYCLING TERMS (1)

1. What is the main body of riders in a race called?
2. What is a 'crevaison'?
3. What is a 'domestique'?
4. What is a 'palmarès'?
5. What is a 'criterium'?
6. What is the 'Broom Wagon'?
7. If there are crosswinds on the stage, what might form in the peloton?
8. If your hands are on the curved part of the handlebars what are you said to be on?
9. What word is used to describe a cyclist's pedal rhythm?
10. What term is used to describe a cyclist who is in a state of utter exhaustion?

QUIZ 6:

CYCLING TERMS (2)

1. What is a 'Fixie'?
2. What is an 'Endo'?
3. What are 'LBS'?
4. What is the padded insert in bicycle shorts called?
5. What are the pair of packs hung over a rear wheel called?
6. What is the term used to describe the distance from the front to rear axle?
7. What is the pocket of air behind a cyclist or vehicle that breaks the wind resistance called?
8. What is a 'track stand'?
9. What is 'fartlek'?
10. What is an 'audax'?

QUIZ 7:
THE GRAND TOURS (1)

1. Name the three Grand Tours.
2. Which of the three Grand Tours started first?
3. In which three months of the year do the three Grand Tours traditionally start?
4. No cyclist has won all three Grand Tours in the same calendar year, but which three riders have won all three in succession (thus holding all titles at the same time)?
5. How many riders have won all three Grand Tours (up to 2020)?
6. Name all the riders who have won all three Grand Tours.
7. The time difference between the winner and second place in the three Grand Tours of 2020 was less than a minute, has this ever happened before?
8. Who, in 1987, became the first person from the southern hemisphere to win a Grand Tour?
9. How many riders have won the Points Classification in all three Grand Tours?
10. Name all the riders who have won the Points Classification in all three Grand Tours.

QUIZ 8:

THE GRAND TOURS (2)

1. Only 35 riders have finished all three Grand Tours in one season, how many times did Australian, Adam Hansen, achieve this feat?
2. How many Grand Tour stage wins did Freddy Maertens take in the 1977 season?
3. Which rider has won the most Points Classifications at the Grand Tours (up to 2020)?
4. How many riders have won the Mountains Classification in all three Grand Tours?
5. Name the riders who have won the Mountains Classification in all three Grand Tours.
6. Which two riders have won the most Young Rider Classifications at the Grand Tours?
7. How many riders have won stages in all three Grand Tours in the same season?
8. Name the riders who have won stages in all three Grand Tours in the same season.
9. How many Grand Tour stage wins did Eddy Merckx take during his career?
10. Name the rider who has the most participations and finishes in Grand Tour history.

QUIZ 9:

TOUR DE FRANCE – GENERAL (1)

1. The first Tour de France in 1903 started outside which café?
2. How many riders started the first Tour?
3. Often referred to as 'Le Grande Boucle', what is the literal translation into English?
4. What position does the 'Lantern Rouge' hold in the race?
5. In what year was the publicity caravan that travels in front of the race introduced?
6. Which two riders hold the record for the most stage wins?
7. Which French rider was King of the Mountains a record seven times?
8. After Paris, which French city has hosted the most starts and finishes?
9. The 'Souvenir Henri Desgranges' is awarded to the rider who does what?
10. In what year was the Polka Dot jersey introduced for the leader in the Mountains Classification?

QUIZ 10:
TOUR DE FRANCE – GENERAL (2)

1. Name the four riders who have won the Tour five times.
2. How many times has Spain hosted the Grand Depart?
3. In what famous sporting venue did the Tour de France finish between 1903 and 1967?
4. Who, or rather what, is Didi Senft better known as?
5. In what year was the first team time trial stage held?
6. What stunt did Canadian Dave Watson do on the Col du Galibier in 2003?
7. How much did the winner of the 2020 Tour receive as first prize (in Euro)?
8. In what year was the first mountain time trial at the Tour?
9. How many times has Mont Ventoux been used as a summit finish in the Tour?
10. How is the most combative rider in the race identified?

QUIZ 11:

TOUR DE FRANCE: 1903-1937

1. Who, in 1903, was the first winner of the Tour de France?
2. Between 1904 and 1911 how was the overall winner decided?
3. Henri Cornet, the winner of the 1904 Tour, had originally finished in which position on the General Classification?
4. In what year was the first ascent of the Col du Tourmalet?
5. Who was the first rider to reach the summit of the Col du Tourmalet that year?
6. Who, in 1919, became the first rider to wear the Yellow Jersey?
7. The 1922 Tour winner, Firmin Lambot, holds what record?
8. In 1926 the Tour started outside Paris for the first time, which spa town hosted the Grand Depart?
9. Which years did Italian rider, Ottavio Bottechia, win the Tour?
10. Name the two British cyclists who started the Tour in 1937, becoming the first from their country to do so.

QUIZ 12:

TOUR DE FRANCE: 1938-1959

1. Which Italian won the Tour either side of World War II, in 1938 and 1948?
2. In 1942, during World War II, a 'Circuit de France' race, held over 6 stages, was organised, but who was the overall winner?
3. In 1947, who won the first Tour held after World War II?
4. In what year was the first ascent of Mont Ventoux?
5. Who was the first rider to win three consecutive Tours?
6. In 1952, Fausto Coppi became the first winner at the summit of which famous climb?
7. In 1954, the Tour started outside of France for the first time, which country hosted the Grand Depart?
8. Which country won the Team Classification at the 1956 Tour?
9. Who, in 1958, became the first winner at the summit of Mont Ventoux?
10. Which Spanish cyclist, nicknamed 'The Eagle of Toledo', won the General Classification and Yellow Jersey at the 1959 Tour?

QUIZ 13:
TOUR DE FRANCE: 1960s

1. Who had a career-ending crash on the descent of the Col d'Aubisque during the 1960 Tour whilst lying in second place on the General Classification?
2. Which country hosted the Grand Depart of the 1962 Tour?
3. Who won the Points Classification in 1964, 1965 and 1967?
4. In what year did Jacques Anquetil take the last of his Tour de France wins?
5. Who collapsed and died during the ascent of the Mont Ventoux on the thirteenth stage of the 1967 Tour?
6. What became mandatory during the 1968 Tour?
7. Raymond Poulidour finished second on GC three times, but how many times did he finish in third place?
8. Where did the Tour finish for the first time in 1968?
9. What feat did Eddy Merckx achieve in the 1969 Tour that has never been equalled?
10. Which British rider won two stages at the 1969 Tour?

QUIZ 14:

TOUR DE FRANCE: 1970s

1. Which city hosted the Grand Depart of the 1970 Tour?
2. Which Spanish rider crashed on the descent of the Col de Menté whilst leading the General Classification of the 1971 Tour?
3. Who won Stage 11 of the 1972 Tour to Mont Ventoux?
4. How many Individual Time Trials were there in the 1973 Tour?
5. Which team won the Team Classification at the 1974 Tour?
6. What happened to Eddy Merckx during Stage 14 of the 1975 Tour?
7. To the nearest hundred, how many miles was the 1977 Tour?
8. Which rider won the Points Classification at the 1978 Tour?
9. Which team won both Team Time Trials at the 1979 Tour?
10. In what year was the first stage finish on the Champs Élysées?

QUIZ 15:
TOUR DE FRANCE: 1980s

1. Who won the 1980 Tour de France?
2. How many stages did Belgian rider, Freddy Maertens, win at the 1981 Tour?
3. Who won an Individual Time Trial to the Puy De Dôme on Stage 15 of the 1983 Tour?
4. Name the Colombian rider who won the Mountains Classification at the 1985 and 1987 Tours.
5. Which city hosted the Grand Depart in 1987?
6. Why was Greg Lemond unable to defend his title in 1987?
7. Which Irishman won the 1987 Tour?
8. Who won the Young Rider Classification at the 1988 Tour?
9. In which ski town did Miguel Indurain take his first ever Tour stage victory during the 1989 Tour?
10. What was the margin of victory when Greg Lemond beat Laurent Fignon in the 1989 Tour?

QUIZ 16:
TOUR DE FRANCE: 1990s

1. Stage 5 from Avranches to Rouen in the 1990 Tour was the last time that a Tour de France stage exceeded what distance?
2. Which team won the Team Time Trial stage at the 1991 Tour?
3. Which terrorist organisation threatened the start of the 1992 Tour when it blew up a French television vehicle?
4. What caused the Belgian cyclist, Wilfried Nelissen, to crash at the end of Stage 1 of the 1994 Tour?
5. What event was the 1994 Tour celebrating when it held 2 stages in the south of England?
6. The 1996 Tour was somewhat of a homecoming race for the great Miguel Indurain but which famous bull running city does he hail from?
7. Which city hosted the Grand Depart in 1997?
8. Which French rider won Stage 5 of the 1997 Tour with a solo 147km breakaway?
9. Why was Belgian rider, Tom Steels, disqualified from the 1997 Tour?
10. Which team withdrew from the 1998 Tour in disgrace following a doping scandal?

QUIZ 17:
TOUR DE FRANCE: 2000s

1. Which rider won the Mountains Classification at the 2001 and 2002 Tours?
2. In the 2003 Tour, Lance Armstrong went "cross-country" to avoid which riders' crash?
3. What was unique about the stage to Alpe d'Huez in the 2004 Tour?
4. Which French rider held the Yellow Jersey for 10 days during the 2004 Tour and repeated the feat in the 2011 Tour?
5. Who won the final stage of the 2005 Tour on the Champs-Élysées with a daring attack from 2km to go?
6. Who was awarded victory in the 2006 Tour following the disqualification of Floyd Landis for failing a doping test?
7. The UK hosted the Grand Depart in 2007, where did Stage 1 finish?
8. In which town did Mark Cavendish take his first Tour de France stage victory in 2008?
9. Which rider won the 2008 Tour?
10. Which climb hosted the last summit finish of the 2009 Tour?

QUIZ 18:

TOUR DE FRANCE: 2010-2020

1. During Stage 9 of the 2011 Tour, which rider crashed, landing on a barbed wire fence, after his breakaway companion Juan Antonio Flecha was hit by a French TV car?
2. Who became the first Australian to win the Tour in 2011?
3. How many stage wins did Peter Sagan take at the 2012 Tour?
4. Which team won the Team Classification at the 2013 Tour?
5. Who won the Young Rider Classification at the 2014 Tour?
6. Which British rider won Stage 14 of the 2015 Tour into Mende?
7. Why was the summit finish at Mont Ventoux in 2016 shortened by 6km, with the stage finishing at Chalet Reynard instead?
8. How many sectors of cobblestones (pavé) were included in Stage 9 of the 2018 Tour?
9. Who won the Combativity Award at the end of the 2018 Tour?
10. Which Irish rider won the Green Jersey at the 2020 Tour?

QUIZ 19:
GIRO D'ITALIA (1)

1. In what year was the first edition of the race held?
2. Who was the winner of the first Giro?
3. What title is given to the highest peak in the race?
4. In the Giro of 1930, why did the organisers pay 22.500 lira to Italian cyclist, Alfredo Binda?
5. In what year was Mount Etna first used as a summit finish?
6. Who, in 1988, became the first Non-European winner of the Giro?
7. Which rider won the 1994 Giro?
8. How many Giro stages did Mario Cipollini win throughout his career?
9. The Monte Zoncolan first appeared in the 2003 Giro, who won the stage that day and went onto repeat the feat when the Giro returned there four years later?
10. Which climb, first used in the 2005 Giro, is not asphalted for the last 7.9km before the summit?

QUIZ 20:

GIRO D'ITALIA (2)

1. The 'Cima Pantani' is awarded to the first rider to the top of which mountain pass?
2. What caused several riders to crash at the finish on Stage 11 of the 2007 Giro?
3. Who won Stage 20 of the 2009 Giro, which was a summit finish on Mount Vesuvius?
4. Stage 7 of the 2010 Giro saw the introduction of Tuscany's famous Strade Blanche (White Roads) into the race, on a wet and muddy day who came out victorious?
5. Race number 108 was retired from use following the tragic death of which rider during the 2011 Giro?
6. By how many points did Joaquim Rodriguez beat Mark Cavendish to win the Points Classification at the 2012 Giro?
7. In 2014 the Giro started with a Team Time Trial in Belfast, which team won the stage?
8. Which country hosted the Giro's Grande Partenza in 2018?
9. How many stage wins did British rider, Simon Yates, take in the 2018 Giro?
10. Which company organised the Giro d'Italia 2020?

QUIZ 21:
VUELTA A ESPAÑA (1)

1. In what year was the first edition of the Vuelta (Tour of Spain)?
2. What colour is the Leader's jersey at the Vuelta?
3. Which rider has taken the most overall wins at the Vuelta?
4. Who is the oldest General Classification winner at the Vuelta?
5. Which rider has the most participations in the Vuelta?
6. Which rider has taken the most Vuelta stage victories?
7. How long is the Sierra Nevada climb, to the nearest kilometre or mile?
8. What colour are the dots on the Mountains Classification jersey?
9. In what year did the Vuelta last visit the Canary Islands?
10. In what year did the Vuelta last visit the Balearic Islands?

QUIZ 22:
VUELTA A ESPAÑA (2)

1. How many riders took part in the 1941 Vuelta?
2. In what year was the Alto de l'Angliru first used?
3. Which French rider won Stage 17 to Luz Ardiden in the 1995 Vuelta?
4. In the 2002 Vuelta, what did David Millar do one metre from the finish line at the top of the Angliru?
5. Which famous motor racing circuit hosted the start of the 2009 Vuelta?
6. In 2011, the Vuelta returned to which region for the first time in 33 years?
7. Antonio Piedra won Stage 15 of the 2012 Vuelta to Lagos de Covadonga, it was the first and only stage victory in the race to date for which team?
8. Which bullring provided the finishing venue to the opening stage of the 2012 Vuelta?
9. Why were Russian, Ivan Rovny, and Italian, Gianluca Brambilla, disqualified from the 2014 Vuelta?
10. What caused the Jumbo Visma team to crash during the Team Time Trial at the 2019 Vuelta?

QUIZ 23:
MILAN SAN REMO (1)

1. In what year was Milan San Remo first held?
2. Who won the first edition of the race?
3. What is traditionally the first climb of the race?
4. On what San Remo street does the race finish?
5. What weather event affected the 1910 race?
6. Who was the first Italian winner of the race?
7. Who had a record 11 podium finishes, 6 times as winner?
8. Which rider won the race in 1968?
9. What are traditionally the last two climbs on the route?
10. Milan San Remo is one of the five monuments, name the other four.

QUIZ 24:

MILAN SAN REMO (2)

1. Who won the race in 1988 and 1989?
2. What climb was added to the race between 2008 and 2014?
3. Who won the race four times between 1997 and 2001?
4. By what distance did Mark Cavendish beat Heinrich Haussler when he won in 2009?
5. Which rider won the race in 2013?
6. Which climb was added to the route in September 2013, only to be removed a few weeks before the race, after the climb had been damaged by landslides?
7. Who, in 2017, became the first Polish winner of the race?
8. In what month was the race held in 2020?
9. A women's race called the Primavera Rosa was held between 1999 and what year?
10. Who was the only rider to win the Primavera Rosa twice?

QUIZ 25:
TOUR OF FLANDERS (1)

1. In what year was the Tour of Flanders first held?
2. Who won the first edition of the race?
3. Who is the youngest winner of the race?
4. Who is the oldest winner of the race?
5. How many times did the great Eddy Merckx win the race?
6. In which city did the race start between 1998 and 2016?
7. What is the average gradient on the Paterberg?
8. What is the maximum gradient on the steepest climb of the race, the Koppenberg?
9. What would you find at the top of the Muur van Geraardsbergen?
10. When the race finished in Meerbeke, which climbs were traditionally the last three on the route?

QUIZ 26:

TOUR OF FLANDERS (2)

1. Who won the race three years in a row between 1949 and 1951?
2. Which British cyclist won the race in 1961?
3. Which Dutchman won the race in 1979 and 1983?
4. Who won the race in 1993, 1995 and 1998?
5. Who won the fastest edition of the race in 2001 with an average speed of 43.6km/h?
6. Which Belgian champion won the race in the years 2008 and 2009?
7. Where did the 2020 race start?
8. The 2020 winner was the son of the 1986 winner, but can you name them?
9. Who are the only two riders to win the Cobbled Classics Double of Paris Roubaix and the Tour of Flanders in the same year twice?
10. Name the five riders who won the race as World Champions.

QUIZ 27:
PARIS-ROUBAIX (1)

1. In what year was Paris-Roubaix first held?
2. Who won the first edition of the race?
3. How much did the winner of the inaugural event receive in prize money?
4. Name the two Roubaix textile manufacturers who created the race.
5. Who is the oldest winner of the race?
6. Which country has produced the most winners?
7. Which two riders jointly hold the record for the most wins in Paris-Roubaix?
8. In which town has the race started since 1977?
9. Also, since 1977, what prize does the winner receive?
10. Where has the race finished since 1989?

QUIZ 28:

PARIS-ROUBAIX (2)

1. Traditionally the first sector of cobblestones (pavé) starts in which town?
2. What is the name of the forest, containing a tricky sector of pavé, which the race passes through?
3. Each sector of pavé is given a difficulty rating between one and five stars, one being the easiest and 5 being the hardest, what is the last five-star sector of the race called?
4. The final stretch of pavé is named after which former winner?
5. Which Italian won the race in 1966?
6. Which Irishman won the race twice in the 1980s?
7. Which team had three of its riders on the podium in the centenary year, 1996?
8. Who, in 2007, became the first Australian to win the race?
9. Which Belgian cyclist had a cardiac arrest during the 2018 race and would become the first fatality in the history of the event?
10. What three events have prevented the race from being run?

QUIZ 29:
LIÈGE-BASTOGNE-LIÈGE (1)

1. In what year was Liège-Bastogne-Liège first held?
2. Which newspaper organised the first race?
3. How many riders finished the first edition of the race?
4. Why was the winner in 1909, Eugène Charlier, disqualified?
5. Where did the first three editions of the race start and finish?
6. Who has won the most Liège-Bastogne-Liège titles?
7. In 1919, 1957, 1980 and 2016 what weather event affected the race?
8. Why were joint winners declared in the 1957 running of the event?
9. How many riders have won the Ardennes Classics (Liège and Flèche Wallonne) in the same year?
10. Name the riders who have won the Ardennes Classics in the same year.

QUIZ 30:
LIÈGE-BASTOGNE-LIÈGE (2)

1. What is the average gradient on the Côte de Stockeu climb?
2. How long, in kilometres or miles, is the Côte du Rosier climb?
3. Between 1998 and 2018 which steep climb was included in the final kilometres of the route?
4. Which American rider won the race in 2003?
5. Which Australian rider won the race in 2014?
6. What was controversial about Alexander Vinokourov's win in the 2010 race?
7. In 2011, what feat did Philippe Gilbert achieve when he won the race?
8. In 2016, what did the organisers include between the top of the final climb and the finish line?
9. In what year was the first women's Liège-Bastogne-Liège held?
10. Who won the women's race in 2019?

QUIZ 31:
TOUR OF LOMBARDY (1)

1. In what year was the Tour of Lombardy, or Il Lombardia, first held?
2. Who won the inaugural race?
3. The Tour of Lombardy is usually held in which month?
4. The race is nicknamed the 'Classica Delle Foglie Morte', what does that translate to in English?
5. The route traditionally winds its way around which Italian lake?
6. In which town did the race finish between 1995 and 2003?
7. In which Swiss town did the race start between 2004 and 2006?
8. In which town did the race finish between 2011 and 2013?
9. Which climb, with a maximum gradient of 27%, was reintroduced in the 2010 edition?
10. Which climb has a church incorporating a cycling museum at the top?

QUIZ 32:

TOUR OF LOMBARDY (2)

1. Who won the race in 1936, 1939 and 1940?
2. Which British rider won the race in 1965?
3. Which Swiss rider won the race in 1998?
4. Damiano Cunego won the race three times, in which years was he victorious?
5. Who was the winner in 2006, five days after his brother had died in a car accident?
6. Which Swiss rider won the race in 2011?
7. Which rider holds the record for the most wins in the race?
8. Which two riders are the only non-Italian riders to win the race three times?
9. How many riders have won both Milan San Remo and the Tour of Lombardy at least once in their career?
10. Which two riders have won 'La Tripletta', which is Milan San Remo, The Tour of Lombardy, and the Giro d'Italia, in the same year?

QUIZ 33:
THE UCI WORLD TOUR (1)

1. Willunga Hill is the key summit finish in which UCI World Tour race?
2. In which Italian city does the Strade Bianche one day race finish?
3. Which is the only UCI World Tour race named after a newspaper?
4. In what year was the first Paris-Nice held?
5. Which rider won the GP de Montréal in 2019?
6. The Flèche Wallonne one day race finishes at the top of which steep hill?
7. What does the winner of the Tour of the Basque Country traditionally wear on the podium?
8. The Tour of the Benelux, or Binckbank Tour, was first held in what year?
9. Which cobbled climb do the riders tackle twice in Gent-Wevelgem?
10. Which rider won the 2020 Tirreno-Adriatico race?

QUIZ 34:
THE UCI WORLD TOUR (2)

1. Which rider has won the most Paris-Nice titles?
2. In which city does the Tour of Poland traditionally finish?
3. Which rider won the 2013 Tour of Catalunya?
4. Which Manx rider became the first Brit to win a stage on Alpe d'Huez, during the 2017 Criterium du Dauphine?
5. What is peculiar about the Three Days of Bruges-De Panne race?
6. In which town does the Bretagne Classic Ouest-France race finish?
7. Which riders' death at the 2003 Paris-Nice race prompted cycling authorities to make helmet use compulsory?
8. The Great Ocean Road Race was first held in 2015 as a farewell race for which rider?
9. Which UCI World Tour race was first held in 2019?
10. Which rider has won the most Tours Down Under?

QUIZ 35:
OTHER UCI TOUR RACES (1)

1. Green Mountain is a decisive summit finish in which UCI Asia Tour race?
2. Which rider won the most Tour of Qatar titles?
3. In what year was the first edition of Paris-Tours?
4. What is peculiar about the Four Days of Dunkirk race?
5. Who won the first edition of the Tour of Yorkshire in 2015?
6. In which country is the annual Tour of Qinghai Lake held?
7. Which Spanish rider won the Brabantse Pijl one day race for three years in a row between 2005 and 2007?
8. The Genting Highlands is a feature in which race?
9. Who won the 2020 Japan Cup?
10. In 1997 what unexpectedly joined the peloton during the Critérium International race?

QUIZ 36:

OTHER UCI TOUR RACES (2)

1. Who won the Volta Ao Algarve (Tour of the Algarve) race in 2011 and 2013?
2. In 2015, Tinkoff-Saxo rider, Jay McCarthy, lost time during a crucial Time Trial at the Tour of Denmark after what interrupted his ride?
3. Which American rider was the first winner of the Tour of Qinghai Lake in 2002?
4. Up until 2016, what was the Tour of the Alps originally known as?
5. Who was the winner of the 2019 Vuelta a San Juan, part of the UCI America Tour?
6. Over how many days is the Three Days of Bruges-De-Panne stage race held?
7. In what year was the last edition of the Critérium International race held?
8. Which UCI Europe Tour race is the oldest still-existing cycling event in Flanders?
9. Who won the inaugural Arctic Race of Norway in 2013?
10. What was remarkable about Iljo Keisse's breakaway win in Stage 7 of the 2012 Tour of Turkey?

QUIZ 37:
THE UCI ROAD WORLD CHAMPIONSHIPS (1)

1. In what country were the first UCI Road World Championships held?
2. Initially the event was only contested by amateurs, who won the first Men's Road Race for Professionals in 1927?
3. What is the name of the jersey awarded to the winners in each UCI Road World Championship race?
4. Which country has won the most medals at the UCI Road World Championships?
5. In total, how many Road and Individual Time Trial World Titles did Jeannie Longo win?
6. Prior to Remco Evenepoel in 2022, who was the last rider to win a Grand Tour and be crowned World Champion in the same year?
7. In what year were the UCI Road World Championships last held in Switzerland?
8. If a rider wins the 'Triple Crown of Cycling' what events have they won?
9. How many riders have achieved the Triple Crown of Cycling?
10. Name the riders who have achieved the Triple Crown of Cycling.

QUIZ 38:

THE UCI ROAD WORLD CHAMPIONSHIPS (2)

1. Who won the Men's Individual Time Trial at the 1994 UCI Road World Championships in Agrigento, Italy?
2. Who won the Men's Road Race at the 1997 UCI Road World Championships held in San Sebastian, Spain?
3. Who was Men's World Individual Time Trial Champion three years in a row between 2003 and 2005?
4. In which city did Manx sprinter, Mark Cavendish, become World Road Race Champion in 2011?
5. The Team Time Trial (TTT) was re-introduced in 2012, which team won the Men's TTT in 2014 and 2015?
6. Peter Sagan was World Champion three years in a row, name the locations where he won his World titles.
7. The Men's Individual Time Trial at the 2017 UCI Road World Championships finished at the top of which steep climb?
8. In what year was the Women's Road Race introduced into the UCI Road World Championships?
9. Who won the Women's Road Race at the 1960 and 1967 UCI Road World Championships?
10. In which country are the 2025 UCI Road World Championships due to be held?

QUIZ 39:
THE OLYMPICS (1)

1. Which Dutch cyclist suffered a horrific crash with just 7 miles to go in the Women's Road Race at the 2016 Rio Olympics?
2. Which sports car manufacturer produced the bike with which Chris Boardman won the Men's Individual Pursuit race at the 1992 Barcelona Olympics?
3. At which Olympics was BMX racing introduced?
4. Up to 2021, which nation has won the most medals in cycling since the Olympics began in 1896?
5. At which Olympics were professional cyclists first allowed to enter?
6. Who won the Men's Road Race at the 2012 London Olympics?
7. Which Dutch cyclist won the first ever Olympic Gold medal in Mountain Biking at the 1996 Atlanta Olympics?
8. Name the Olympic Gold Medal winner who suffered a fatal crash on the descent of the Col de Portet d'Aspet at the 1995 Tour de France.
9. Which American cyclist won Gold in the Women's Road Race at the 1984 Los Angeles Olympics?
10. Which British rider won the Bronze medal in the Men's Road Race at the 1996 Atlanta Olympics?

QUIZ 40:
THE OLYMPICS (2)

1. Who won Gold in the Men's Individual Time Trial at both the 2000 Sydney Olympics and the 2004 Athens Olympics?
2. How many Gold medals has British Paralympian, Sarah Storey, won during her career?
3. Which rider took the last win of his career at the 1996 Atlanta Olympics in the Men's Individual Time Trial?
4. At which Olympics was the Individual Pursuit introduced?
5. In what event did British cyclist, Peter Kennaugh, win Gold at the 2012 London Olympics, becoming the first Gold medallist from the Isle of Man in 100 years?
6. Who won the Gold medal in the Women's BMX at both the 2012 and 2016 Games?
7. Which country won the Men's Team Time Trial on the road at the 1992 Barcelona Olympics?
8. Before winning Gold on the track at the 2008 Beijing Olympics, British cyclist Rebecca Romero had won silver four years earlier in Athens, but in which sport?
9. Who won the Women's Individual Time Trial at the 2008, 2012 and 2016 Olympics?
10. Who won Gold in the Men's Road Race at the first Olympics in 1896?

QUIZ 41:
BRITISH CYCLING (1)

1. Who was the first British winner of the Tour de France?
2. Which Scottish cyclist broke the UCI World Hour record twice in the 1990s on a bicycle he built himself which included parts from a washing machine?
3. Which Manx sprinter was known as 'The Pocket Rocket'?
4. Which Scottish cyclist won the King of the Mountains competition at the 1984 Tour de France?
5. Which Welsh rider won Gold in the 2014 Commonwealth Games Men's Road Race held in Glasgow?
6. Who broke the British national 10-mile time trial record in 2016 with a time of 16 minutes 35 seconds?
7. The Manx International Cycling Race took place on which infamous motor-racing circuit?
8. Which Scottish rider was banned for two years in 2004 after he admitted taking performance enhancing drugs?
9. Who writes in Cycling Weekly magazine under the name of Doctor Hutch?
10. Who holds the record for cycling from Land's End to John O'Groats?

QUIZ 42:
BRITISH CYCLING (2)

1. How many British riders have won the Tour de France?
2. Which Scottish cyclist has been eleven times a World Champion and six times an Olympic Champion on the track?
3. Which Manx sprinter is the only British rider to win the Points Classification jerseys at each of the three Grand Tours?
4. Where was Sir Bradley Wiggins born?
5. Who masterminded British Cycling's successes at the 2008 and 2012 Summer Olympics?
6. What year was the first Tour of Britain held?
7. How many times has Edvald Boasson Hagen won the Tour of Britain?
8. Who won the 2017 British National Championships Men's Road Race and Individual Time Trial held on the Isle of Man?
9. Who am I? I was born in Preston in July 1994; I rode for two seasons with the Caja Rural-Seguros RGA Team and in 2020 I won a Vuelta stage at the top of the Alto de l'Angliru?
10. Name the 5 cyclists who have won the BBC Sports Personality of the Year Award.

QUIZ 43:
WOMEN'S CYCLING (1)

1. Which British rider was the first winner of the women's Gent-Wevelgem?
2. Which Cuban rider won the Great Ocean Road Race in 2019?
3. How many times did Dutch cyclists, Marianne Vos and Annemiek Van Vleuten, both win La Course by Le Tour de France?
4. Which American won the first Strade Bianche women's race in 2015?
5. In what year was the Giro d'Italia Femminile, or Giro Rosa, first held?
6. Which British rider won the Tour of Flanders for Women in 2007?
7. Who was the first winner of La Flèche Wallonne Féminine?
8. Up to 2022, which two Dutch riders have the most wins at the women's Liege-Bastogne-Liege?
9. Which Isle of Man cyclist became the first British rider to win a stage of the modern Tour de France Féminin in 1993?
10. Which British rider won La Flèche Wallonne Féminine in 2010?

QUIZ 44:
WOMEN'S CYCLING (2)

1. Who set a women's UCI Hour record of 49.254km in the Tissot Velodrome in Grenchen in May 2022?
2. Who was the first ever women's UCI Cyclo-Cross World Champion in the year 2000?
3. How many times has Marianne Vos been World Champion on the road and in cyclo-cross in the same year?
4. Who, in 1991, was the first women's UCI Mountain Bike World Cup winner?
5. In 2019, what was the World's richest women's race?
6. Who won the 2018 Women's Tour of California?
7. After retiring from cycling, Victoria Pendleton turned her attentions to horse racing. Riding 'Pacha du Polder', what position did she finish in the 2016 Foxhunter Chase at Cheltenham?
8. Who won the Women's Tour of Britain in 2017?
9. Who won the Women's Road Race at the 1987 World Championships in Villach, Austria?
10. Why was the women's 2019 Omloop Het Nieuwsblad race 'neutralised?'

QUIZ 45:
TRACK CYCLING (1)

1. What system is not usually included on a track bike?
2. What is the name of the motorized bicycle that riders follow in the Keirin race?
3. Which German company specialises in the design of velodromes designing more than 125 cycle tracks worldwide?
4. What distance must Olympic and World Championship Velodromes measure?
5. What does the white line on a velodrome signify?
6. Where is the World's shortest velodrome?
7. Which is the oldest velodrome still in use?
8. The 1900 UCI Track Cycling World Championships were held in which former velodrome?
9. If you were riding on the Denton Park Velodrome in which country would you be?
10. Since 2016, which four events make up the Omnium?

QUIZ 46:
TRACK CYCLING (2)

1. Which Spanish rider broke the UCI Hour Record in September 1994?
2. Which velodrome hosted the 1995 UCI Track Cycling World Championships?
3. In what year was the UCI Track Cycling World Cup first held?
4. In 2006, Spanish cyclist Isaac Galvez, suffered a fatal crash at which historic track cycling meeting?
5. In what event did Mark Cavendish win Gold for the Isle of Man at the 2006 Commonwealth Games in Melbourne?
6. How many Gold medals did Australian, Anna Meares, win at the 2010 Commonwealth Games in Delhi?
7. Who won Gold in the Men's Sprint at the 2010 UCI Track World Championships in Ballerup, Denmark?
8. What events were removed from the Omnium in 2016?
9. Which Olympic and World Champion was left paralysed after a training accident at the Cottbus Velodrome in June 2018?
10. Which country has taken the most wins at the UCI Track Cycling World Cup?

QUIZ 47:
CYCLO-CROSS (1)

1. The 'Le Critérium International de Cross-Country Cyclo-Pédestre' was the first international race in cyclo-cross, in what year was it first held?
2. What city staged the first UCI Cyclo-Cross World Championships?
3. In what year was the first UCI Cyclo-Cross World Championships held?
4. What technique did Danny De Bie use to overcome obstacles such as barriers and ditches during his successful World Championship run in 1989?
5. Which country hosted the 1999 UCI Cyclo-Cross World Championships?
6. Who was the women's UCI Cyclo-Cross World Champion in 2015, completing a unique 'Triple Crown' having been crowned World Champion in Mountain Biking and on the Road during the previous 12 months?
7. In what year was the Men's DVV-Trophy, previously known as the BPost Bank Trophy, first held?
8. Who won the Men's DVV-Trophy in the 2019-2020 season?
9. In which English County is the 61km Three Peaks Cyclo-Cross Race held annually?
10. In which American city is the Cyclocross Crusade held?

QUIZ 48:
CYCLO-CROSS (2)

1. How many rounds does the UCI Cyclo-Cross Superprestige competition consist of?
2. Which male rider has taken the most UCI Cyclo-Cross Superprestige wins?
3. In what year was the Women's UCI Cyclo-Cross Superprestige competition first held?
4. How many of the eight UCI Cyclo-Cross Superprestige races did Mathieu Van Der Poel win in the 2018-19 season?
5. How many times has Belgian, Sanne Cant, won the Women's UCI Cyclo-Cross Superprestige competition?
6. In what year was the UCI Cyclo-Cross World Cup first staged?
7. Which city hosted the first ever American round of the UCI Cyclo-Cross World Cup in September 2015?
8. Which British rider was Men's Under-23 UCI Cyclo-Cross World Cup winner in the 2017-18 and 2018-19 seasons?
9. Which male cyclist won the UCI World Cup, the UCI Superprestige and was crowned World Champion in the 2009-10 season?
10. The Barry-Roubaix held in Michigan, USA is known as the World's largest gravel road race, in what year was it established?

QUIZ 49:

MOUNTAIN BIKING (1)

1. Who built the first mountain bike frames?
2. In what year were the UCI Mountain Bike World Championships inaugurated?
3. Who was Men's UCI Cross-Country World Champion for four years in a row between 2004 and 2007?
4. Who finished second in the Men's UCI Downhill World Championships Race in the years 2000, 2001, 2002 and 2008 before eventually winning it in 2009?
5. Which Isle of Man TT rider and TV celebrity finished the 2712-mile Tour Divide race in 2016?
6. How many times have the UCI Mountain Bike World Championships been held in Canada?
7. Who won the Men's Cross-Country at the 1999 UCI World Championships before turning his attentions to the Tour de France, where he was King of the Mountains in 2005 and 2006?
8. Which rider won the Women's Cross-Country race at the 2011 and 2014 UCI World Championships?
9. In which town were the UCI Mountain Bike World Championships held in 2007?
10. Who won the Men's Downhill at the 2020 UCI World Championships in Leogang, Austria?

QUIZ 50:

MOUNTAIN BIKING (2)

1. Which country held the first round of the UCI Mountain Bike World Cup in 2009?
2. In what year was the company 'Camelbak Products, LLC' founded?
3. Who was Women's UCI Downhill World Champion every year between 1996 and 2003, and then again in 2005?
4. Which British rider was Women's UCI Downhill World Champion in 2010?
5. The MCR Descender is credited as the World's first rear suspension mountain bike, but who invented it?
6. What team does Swiss cyclist, Nino Schurter, race for?
7. Which rider won the Men's UCI Downhill World Cup in 2017?
8. Which British rider has been Women's UCI Downhill World Champion five times?
9. How long does the Mountain Mayhem race, held annually in the UK, last?
10. In 2021, Canadian cyclist, Emily Batty, left Subaru-Trek to race for which team?

QUIZ 51:
BMX (1)

1. In what year were the first UCI BMX World Championships held?
2. In what year did BMX become an Olympic sport?
3. Which BMX discipline was introduced at the 2020 Tokyo Olympics?
4. Where were the 2018 UCI BMX World Championships held?
5. In what year was the American Bicycle Association established?
6. In 1980, which town installed the UK's first BMX track?
7. In what year was the International BMX Federation founded?
8. Who was the first Men's Olympic BMX Champion?
9. What is a step-up jump?
10. Who created the United Kingdom Bicycle Motocross Association in 1980?

QUIZ 52:
BMX (2)

1. In 1969, where was the first known BMX race held?
2. What make and model of bike was involved in the first known race?
3. In what year was the National Bicycle League started?
4. Who was the Elite Men's UCI BMX World Champion in 1996 and 2001?
5. Who was the Elite Women's UCI BMX World Champion in 2013?
6. Which two countries have won the most medals at the UCI BMX World Championships?
7. In what year, were the UCI BMX World Championships held in Adelaide?
8. In what year was the first UCI BMX Supercross World Cup held?
9. Who was the winner of the Men's UCI BMX Supercross World Cup in 2014 and 2015?
10. Who won the Women's UCI BMX Supercross World Cup every year between 2016 and 2019?

QUIZ 53:
GRAN FONDO / CYCLOSPORTIVE (1)

1. In what year did the UCI Gran Fondo World Series start?
2. If you were riding up the Molenberg, which sportive might you be taking part in?
3. The route of the Tour Ride sportive in the UK goes through the estate of a famous ceramic art company, which one?
4. In which Spanish town does the Gran Fondo Quebrantahuesos start and finish?
5. In what year was the L'Étape du Tour first held?
6. Who was the first winner of L'Étape du Tour?
7. In 1982 the first ever French sportive was established, what is it called?
8. If you were taking part in the Lake Taupo Cycle Challenge, in which country would you be?
9. What is unique about the L'Eroica sportive in Italy?
10. Name the six new rounds that were added to the UCI Gran Fondo World Series in 2021.

QUIZ 54:
GRAN FONDO / CYCLOSPORTIVE (2)

1. The King Ridge Gran Fondo in North America was founded by which former professional cyclist?
2. Who was the winner of the Maratona dles Dolomites Gran Fondo in the year 2000?
3. What are the three mountain passes featured in the Time-Megève-Mont Blanc sportive?
4. The Drumgoff Climb on the 'Wicklow 200' sportive has a monument to which Irish cyclist at the top?
5. The first ever Gran Fondo, the Nove Colli, was held in which year?
6. How many stages are there in the Tour of Crete sportive, held since 2016?
7. In 2014 what professional race, over 610km (380 miles) was resurrected and held as a cyclosportive?
8. Approximately how many riders took part in the inaugural Prudential RideLondon-Surrey 100 in 2013?
9. On what mythical mountain does La Marmotte finish?
10. Where did the 2018 UCI Gran Fondo World Championships take place?

QUIZ 55:

TRIATHLON (1)

1. What three disciplines make up the triathlon?
2. What is the governing body of triathlon called?
3. In what year was the governing body founded?
4. What is the distance of the cycling leg in a standard triathlon race?
5. In what year was triathlon first included in the Olympics?
6. What do competitors receive if they mount their bike inside the designated transition area?
7. In what year did the ITU World Triathlon Series start?
8. Which male triathlete has won the most ITU World Triathlon Series titles?
9. Which brothers were first and second in the 2011 and 2012 ITU World Triathlon Series Men's Championship?
10. Who was the winner of the ITU World Triathlon Series three years in a row between 2016 and 2018?

QUIZ 56:

TRIATHLON (2)

1. Which country hosted the first round of the 2014 ITU World Triathlon Series?
2. Who won the ITU World Triathlon Series Women's Championship in 2019?
3. In what year was the first ITU Triathlon World Cup?
4. Who won the Men's ITU Triathlon World Cup in 1998?
5. Who won the Women's ITU Triathlon World Cup in 2005?
6. Where does the Enduroman Arch to Arc triathlon start and finish?
7. Which company organises the Ironman and the Ironman 70.3 races?
8. Where is the annual Ironman World Championships held?
9. What is the distance of the cycling leg in an Ironman triathlon race?
10. Who was the ITU Long Distance Triathlon World Champion in 2017?

QUIZ 57:
SPONSORS (1)

1. What type of products does the German sponsor, Alpecin, manufacture?
2. In what year was 'Ineos' founded?
3. What kind of services did 'Banesto' provide?
4. What does Italian manufacturer, Mapei, produce?
5. Which coffee company has been a team sponsor since 2016?
6. What is 'Jean Delatour?'
7. 'AG2R' is associated with which line of business?
8. What is 'Amore & Vita?'
9. Which Belgian manufacturer of windows and doors was secondary sponsor to the Lotto team between 2012 and 2014?
10. In 2013 the Rabobank name was removed and replaced with what word whilst Rabobank continued to fulfil its contractual obligations to fund the squad through the 2013 season?

QUIZ 58:
SPONSORS (2)

1. Team Vacansoleil were co-sponsored by DCM, what do DCM produce?
2. One of Mario Cipollini's teams was sponsored by an Italian hotel chain, what were they called?
3. What is Italian manufacturer 'Faema' known for producing?
4. 'La Française des Jeux' is what?
5. 'Fynsec' was co-sponsor of Jacques Anquetil's Helyett squad between 1959 and 1961 but what did they produce?
6. Which Australian fertilizer maker were title sponsor and then co-sponsor of the Orica team between 2012 and 2017?
7. 'Mercatone Uno' in Italy and 'Casino' in France are what kind of establishments?
8. What did 'Molteni' make before they went bankrupt in 1987?
9. What is O.N.C.E.?
10. Greg Lemond won his third Tour riding for the 'Z' team but what type of company is 'Z'?

QUIZ 59:
BRANDS (1)

Can you name the companies that produce the following products?

1. 'Night Vision' jacket.
2. 'Mojito' road helmet.
3. The 'Aggressor' mountain bike.
4. 'Orhi' bib shorts.
5. 'Jawbreaker' sunglasses.
6. 'Go' and 'Rego' energy drinks.
7. The 'Hummvee' jersey.
8. The official 2021 Trek-Segafredo Cycling Team jersey.
9. 'Supersix Evo' framset.
10. The 'Antares' saddle.

QUIZ 60:

BRANDS (2)

1. In what year was the clothing company, Castelli, founded?
2. Which company produces the 'Genius' range of road shoes?
3. Which company makes 'Chamois Butt'r Eurostyle?'
4. What type of products does the company 'Finish Line' manufacture?
5. In what year was the Bicycle manufacturer, Orbea, founded?
6. Which company produces 'Keo Classic' pedals?
7. Which company makes the 'Nytro' E-Bike?
8. What advertising slogan did the company 'Alpecin' drop for the duration of the Tour de France in 2015?
9. Which company makes the official 2021 Cofidis jersey?
10. In what year was the component's manufacturer, Campagnolo, founded?

QUIZ 61:
NICKNAMES (1)

Can you name the rider, past or present, from their nickname?

1. Big Mig.
2. Il Pirata (The Pirate).
3. The Eagle of Toledo.
4. The Cannibal.
5. The Tourminator.
6. Spartacus.
7. The Lion King.
8. The Lion of Flanders.
9. El Pistolero.
10. The Badger.

QUIZ 62:

NICKNAMES (2)

Can you name the rider, past or present, from their nickname?

1. The Manx Missile.
2. The Scarlet Pimpernel.
3. Il Campionissimo (The Champion).
4. Le Monster.
5. The Professor.
6. Der Kaiser.
7. G.
8. Il Grillo (The Cricket).
9. Il Gladiatore (The Gladiator).
10. Perico.

QUIZ 63:
CYCLING RECORDS (1)

1. Who, in 2018, set a motor-paced speed World record of 296km/h (183.93mph)?
2. Who set a downhill speed record of 227.72km/h (141.50mph), using a prototype bicycle, on the speed snow track at Vars in France in March 2017?
3. Can you name the Belgian rider who set a then men's UCI Hour Record of 55.089km (34.231mi) in 2019?
4. What distance did Chris Boardman ride when he set the farthest distance ever set in a Men's UCI Hour Record attempt in 1996?
5. Which male rider set a new UCI Hour Record of 91.556km (56.89 miles) on a streamlined recumbent bicycle in August 2011?
6. How far did Ralph Disviscourt cycle when he set a new 24-hour road record in Vianden, Luxembourg in July 2020?
7. Who, in 2021, set a Women's record for cycling between Land's End to John O'Groats of 51 hours, 19 minutes and 23 seconds?
8. To the nearest hour, how many hours did it take Gethin Butler to cycle 1000 miles in 2001?
9. How many of cycling's monuments did Eddy Merckx win?
10. Which rider has won the most Vélo d'Or awards?

QUIZ 64:
CYCLING RECORDS (2)

1. Which male rider won the most UCI Road World Cups?
2. How many hours did Kurt Osborn spend on one wheel when he set the Guinness World Record for the longest bicycle wheelie in August 1998?
3. 'The Man Who Cycled the World' book and BBC television programme tells the story of which cyclists attempt to break the Guinness World Record for a Circumnavigational Bike Tour of the World?
4. Which rider set a 4000m Individual Pursuit record of 4:01.934 at the 2020 UCI Track World Championships?
5. Which female rider set a Flying 500m Time Trial record of 28.970 on the track in December 2016?
6. Who, in 2014, set the record for the fastest average speed of 16.42mph (26.425km) in the Race Across America?
7. To the nearest mph, what average speed did Seana Hogan achieve when she set a new Race Across America record in 1995?
8. What extraordinary feat did German cyclist, Jens Stotzer, achieve in 2013?
9. In 1998, Kurt Osbourn set the record for the longest bicycle wheelie. How many hours did he ride on one wheel?
10. In 2017, Jasmijn Muller set a non-stop distance record of 18.28km in which virtual World?

QUIZ 65:
KING OF THE MOUNTAINS (1)

1. What is the name of the famous climb in the Clasica de San Sebastian that often proves to be the decisive point in the race?
2. The Tour of California is often decided on which summit finish?
3. How many hairpin bends are there on the mythical Alpe d'Huez?
4. The climb of Holme Moss often features in which race?
5. Where would you be if you were taking on the Snaefell Mountain Course?
6. Which climb has the highest maximum gradient, the Alto de l'Angliru or the Monte Zoncolan?
7. Who holds the record for the fastest ascent of Alpe d'Huez, with a time of 37 minutes 30 seconds in the 2010 Criterium Du Dauphine?
8. The Passo di Stelvio is in which country?
9. What is the highest peak ever used in the Tour de France?
10. The summit of the Col du Portillon forms the border between which two countries?

QUIZ 66:

KING OF THE MOUNTAINS (2)

1. Starting at Bagnères-de-Luchon, what is the distance to the summit of the Col de Peyresourde (to the nearest kilometre or mile)?
2. In which race is the summit finish of 'Laguna de Neila' a regular feature?
3. Which one-day race finishes at the top of the Cauberg?
4. What is the highest peak in Austria and often used as a summit finish in the Tour of Austria?
5. The Urkiola climb in Northern Spain was the focus of the Subida Urkiola one-day race between 1931 and 2009, but who won the race the last time it was held?
6. What was unusual about Chris Froome's ascent of the Mont Ventoux in the 2016 Tour?
7. What is the maximum gradient on the Col du Galibier?
8. How high, in metres, is the Monte Zoncolan?
9. The 'Arrate' summit finish features regularly in which stage race?
10. What is the name of the town at the foot of the Alpe d'Huez?

QUIZ 67:
GEOGRAPHY (1)

1. Which State Capitol provided the venue for the final stage of the USA Pro Cycling Challenge, held between 2011 and 2015?
2. Which two one-day races are Canada's only events on the UCI World Tour?
3. In which country would you be riding if you were on the Causeway Coastal Route?
4. In which state is the Tour Down Under held?
5. The Tour of Flanders museum is in which Belgian town?
6. What is the name of the famous avenue in Tours where the Paris-Tours race finished up until 2011?
7. In which country is the Cape Epic mountain bike race held?
8. If you were cycling from Helsingør to Fredensborg, what country would you be in?
9. The Great Ocean Road Race starts and finishes in Cadel Evans' hometown, what is it called?
10. Which classic one-day race finishes by the beautiful Playa de la Concha beach?

QUIZ 68:
GEOGRAPHY (2)

1. The Tramuntana Mountains are a popular holiday destination for cyclists, but where can they be found?
2. The Ruta de los Conquistadores is an off-road cycle route in which country?
3. If you were in Tromsø what UCI Europe Tour race might you be watching?
4. Which country would you be in if you were cycling over the River Ebro?
5. In which French city is the start point of the Canal du Midi?
6. Mount Teide is a popular training destination for pro-cyclists, but on which island is it located?
7. In which British city would you find the Sir Chris Hoy Velodrome?
8. Where does the Tour of the Gila traditionally start?
9. What can be found at the top of the Madonna del Ghisallo near Lake Como?
10. The Grand Old Duke of York marched his men to the top of a hill in Northern France which provides the setting for the decisive stage in the Four Days of Dunkirk bike race, what is the town called that sits on top of the hill?

QUIZ 69:

LANDMARKS (1)

1. Which well-known art gallery does the Tour De France peloton pass on the final stage of the race in Paris?
2. The Tour De France sometimes passes the Millau Viaduct, in what year was the viaduct opened?
3. Traditionally the final stage of the Tour Down Under passes which cricket ground?
4. Which UCI World Tour stage race passes the Wawel Castle?
5. Which Spanish city, regularly visited by the Vuelta, is noted for its Casas Colgadas, or hanging houses?
6. Which week-long stage race passes the Montjuic Olympic stadium?
7. Which famous museum did the Vuelta pass when it had a stage finish in Bilbao?
8. What venue in Verona was used to host the final stage of the Giro in 2019?
9. Which Italian hill-top town, said to be the birthplace of St Francis, is noted for its basilica and a spectacular stage victory by Joaquim Rodriguez in the 2012 Giro?
10. The finishing circuit for the 2008 Olympics Road Race was at Badaling, what famous landmark would you find there?

QUIZ 70:

LANDMARKS (2)

1. The Vizcaya Bridge provides the backdrop for the start of which race?
2. Where would you be if you were riding past the Hofburg?
3. The Bled Bike Festival, on the shores of Lake Bled, takes place in which country?
4. Which race finishes at the citadel in Namur?
5. Under what famous landmark did the 2003 Tour De France start?
6. Where might you be if you cycle past the Maoi statues?
7. On which Mediterranean island would you be cycling if you passed the Mosta Dome?
8. Mont-St-Michel provided the setting for the Grand Depart of the Tour De France in which year?
9. In which city would you be if you were cycling along the Bosporus and passed the Hagia Sophia?
10. The Canfranc Railway Station features on the route of which cyclosportive?

QUIZ 71:

FOOD AND DRINK (1)

1. Cassoulet is the local speciality in which area of France?
2. Which company produces 'Ride' bars?
3. What is the name given to the food bag handed out to riders during a race by their teams?
4. What does the winner of Paris-Camembert receive as a prize?
5. Which company produces the 'Go' range of nutritional products?
6. Which Spanish soft drinks manufacturer sponsored a team between 1959 and 1979, then again from 1986 to 1988?
7. Mint Cake is an energy-boosting snack associated with which British town?
8. What locally-produced wine might the winner of a race into Logroño drink to celebrate?
9. Which company produced a Summer Pudding flavour energy bar?
10. What drink would you associate with Ename, a small town in Flanders?

QUIZ 72:
FOOD AND DRINK (2)

1. What does Tour sponsor, Cochonou, produce?
2. What confectionery manufacturer sponsors a US pro-cycling team?
3. If you were riding through Cheddar Gorge, what English county would you be in?
4. What did Mark Cavendish receive for winning Stage 1 of the 2015 Presidential Tour of Turkey into Alanya?
5. The Standert Cycling Café is in which European Capital City?
6. McLaren Vale traditionally plays host to the start of the queen stage of the Tour Down Under, what drink is the town noted for producing?
7. On average how many calories does a Tour De France rider burn each day (to the nearest hundred)?
8. What juice can boost stamina and endurance?
9. What reason did Alberto Contador give for failing a doping test during the 2010 Tour De France?
10. Where am I? The year is 2001, the riders are in front of the Belfry, signing on for a classic one-day race and I am wandering the canals whilst eating some locally-produced chocolate.

QUIZ 73:
LITERATURE (1)

1. "Learn to ride a bicycle. You will not regret it if you live." Which author provided us with this as advice?
2. 'The Hour: Sporting Immortality the Hard Way' was written by which former cyclist?
3. Who wrote the book 'Britain By Bike?'
4. Which annual bike race is mentioned and described in Ernest Hemingway's novel 'The Sun Also Rises?'
5. Which cycling commentator released a book entitled 'Magic Spanner?'
6. British travel writer and humourist, Tim Moore, wrote a book about shadow riding the Tour de France, what was it called?
7. Whose autobiography was called 'Racing Through the Dark'?
8. 'The Wheels of Change' was an 1895 book about cycling written by which famous author?
9. Who was the author of 'The Escape Artist: Life from the Saddle?'
10. Which 19th century French author used bicycles in two of his novels, 'Paris' and 'Fruitfulness', to reflect the changing culture of the time and the transformation of the main characters?

QUIZ 74:
LITERATURE (2)

1. In 2014, illustrator Jan Cleijne published a book about which race?
2. 'The Bike Tour Mystery' by Carolyn Keene is the 168th volume in the series of which fictional character?
3. What colour was the bicycle in the title of a book published by author Haifaa Al-Mansour in 2015?
4. 'The Adventure of the Solitary Cyclist' and 'The Adventure of the Priory School' are short stories featuring which fictional private detective?
5. "Life is like riding a bicycle – in order to keep your balance, you must keep moving" who offered these words of wisdom?
6. 'The Racer' is a 1978 book published by which respected Dutch journalist and novelist?
7. Who wrote the book 'Put Me Back on My Bike: In Search of Tom Simpson?'
8. 'Beyond the City', published in 1893, is one of the earliest accounts of the 'bicycle machine' in literature, but who was its author?
9. What was the title of Ned Boulting's first book about cycling?
10. "Nothing compares to the simple pleasure of riding a bike" is a quote from which American President?

QUIZ 75:
AT THE MOVIES (1)

1. Which company made the bicycle that appears in the movie E.T.?
2. 'The Flying Scotsman', released in 2006, is based on the true story of which cyclist?
3. 'Overcoming' is a 2005 documentary film about which Pro Cycling Team?
4. In which 1947 movie do a father and son search for a stolen bicycle in Rome?
5. Who starred as Lance Armstrong in the film, 'The Program?'
6. What was the 1976 film about Paris-Roubaix called?
7. Which Australian actress played Judy in the 1983 movie, BMX Bandits?
8. 'Chasing Legends' was a 2009 documentary film about which Pro Cycling Team?
9. The Tour de France is portrayed in which 2003 animated movie?
10. Which actor played Marcus Sommers in the 1985 movie, American Flyers?

QUIZ 76:
AT THE MOVIES (2)

1. What 1200km trail do Rebecca Rusch and her riding partner Huyen Nguyen follow in the 2017 film, Blood Road?
2. Who plays Jack Casey in the 1985 movie, Quicksilver?
3. 'Inspired to Ride' is a 2015 documentary film about which race?
4. Which Dirty Dancing actress appeared as Leslie in 'American Flyers?'
5. Who directed 'Pee Wee's Big Adventure?'
6. Where do brothers Lachlan and Angus Morton ride to in the film, Thereabouts?
7. Who starred as Mike in the 1979 movie, Breaking Away?
8. Which Monty Python actor crashed his bicycle into the Griswold's car in 'National Lampoon's European Vacation'?
9. In which movie does Joseph Gordon-Levitt play a bicycle messenger operating in New York City?
10. 'Time Trial' is a 2017 documentary film about which Scottish cyclist?

QUIZ 77:
TELEVISION (1)

1. In what year was the first live television coverage of the Tour de France?
2. Which race would you be watching if you heard the theme tune "Feel the Rush, Wheels in Motion?'
3. Which late Eurosport commentator said that it was "Curtains for Karpets" as the rider Vladimir Karpets got dropped on a mountain climb?
4. Which father and son duo took to two wheels in the Channel 5 production 'Britain by Bike?'
5. Which famous English commentator is the voice of NBC Sports Tour de France coverage?
6. Why did France's advertising watchdog ban a TV commercial for the Dutch-made VanMoof Bicycle?
7. In what year did 'The Bike Channel' cease transmission?
8. What did the eco-friendly 'Cottage Lodge' in Brockenhurst, UK, install in one of its guest rooms in 2012?
9. Which Spanish broadcaster provides the coverage for the Vuelta a España?
10. Which former Vuelta a España and Paris-Roubaix winner is a commentator on Eurosport?

QUIZ 78:
TELEVISION (2)

1. Which classic British sitcom has an episode entitled 'Duet for Solo Bicycle?'
2. Mongoose and Schwinn produced limited-edition replicas of bicycles featured in which Netflix series?
3. Who is the host of ITV's 'The Cycle Show?'
4. Which two companies produce the TV coverage of the Tour de France?
5. What is the name of the Eurosport commentator who was British National Champion in 1991 and 1994?
6. In Red Bull TV's 'Ice 2 Ice' programme, Michael Strasser, attempts to set a new World cycling record between which two locations?
7. Which former professional rider and commentator died in December 2018 at his home in Uganda?
8. Who presented the BBC programme 'Britain By Bike?'
9. In 'Speed with Guy Martin' he breaks the British record for speed on a bicycle, to the nearest mph or kmph, what was his top speed?
10. Actor Michael Crawford teamed up with which cyclist for a special 'Some Mothers Do 'Ave 'Em' scene in Sport Relief 2016?

QUIZ 79:
THE MUSIC ROUND (1)

1. Which act had a 2010 hit with 'The Bike Song?'
2. Which Colombian singer released a song with Carlos Vives called 'La Bicicleta?'
3. In what year was 'Bicycle Race' by Queen released?
4. Which German electropop group released an album entitled 'Tour De France?'
5. Who was riding a bike in the video for her 2001 hit, 'Wrong Impression?'
6. Which singer did Lance Armstrong date between 2003 and 2006?
7. How many bicycles were in Beijing in the Katie Melua song?
8. 'Dia Cero' was a song used in a promotional TV advert for which race in 2012?
9. Which singer recorded a song called 'Riding on my bicycle' for 'At Home with The Kids' a charity record released in 2020 for Save The Children?
10. In 2012, which pro cycling team asked you to 'Call Me Maybe' on a YouTube video?

QUIZ 80:

THE MUSIC ROUND (2)

1. What colour was Nazareth's bicycle in their 1975 hit?
2. Who released a single called 'Broken Bicycles' in 1982?
3. Which band had a hit with 'The Pushbike Song' in 1970?
4. 'Bike' is the final song on the debut album of which British rock band?
5. In which Coldplay music video are the band seen riding BMX bikes around Mexico City?
6. Which mountain biker appears on the video for 'Winter Hill', a single released by Doves in 2009?
7. What is the name of the former Talking Heads frontman who published a book in 2010 called 'Bicycle Diaries'?
8. Which act produced 'Theme for Velodrome' for the 2012 London Olympics?
9. In 2012 the lead singer of the Beautiful South, Paul Heaton, cycled to his gigs, what distance did he cover?
10. Complete the lyrics: "All I wanna do is…"

ANSWERS

QUIZ 1: ITS ALL ABOUT THE BIKE (1)

1. 1817; 2. Karl Von Drais; 3. Pinarello (16 wins); 4. Specialized Stumpjumper and Univega Alpina Pro 5. Folding; 6. 1989; 7. Orbea; 8. 1996; 9. Shimano; 10. Marcel Kittel in the 2017 Tour de France.

QUIZ 2: ITS ALL ABOUT THE BIKE (2)

1. Cinelli; 2. Curtis H. Veeder (in 1895); 3. Pinarello; 4. Campagnolo; 5. Colnago; 6. Zwift; 7. Markus Storck; 8. Presta and Schrader; 9. Giant; 10. After a rabbit was reportedly killed by them at a cyclocross race and Paolo Bettini cut his hand in a crash they were deemed too dangerous.

QUIZ 3: THE UCI (1)

1. Union Cycliste Internationale; 2. 1900; 3. Emile de Beukelaer (1900-1922); 4. Aigle, Switzerland; 5. David Lappartient; 6. Thirty; 7. The International Amateur Cycling Federation (FIAC) and The International Professional Cycling Federation (FICP); 8. A velodrome; 9. Compulsory helmet use (the rule was revoked); 10. Tracey Gaudry (in 2013).

QUIZ 4: THE UCI (2)

1. 1989; 2. The UCI ProTour Series; 3. Graeme Obree; 4. 196; 5. The World Anti-Doping Agency (WADA); 6. Patrick McQuaid; 7. Bob Stapleton; 8. The UCI Bike City Label. 9. Landis had accused the body of several misdeeds, including accepting a bribe from Lance Armstrong to cover up an EPO positive after the 2001 Tour of Switzerland; 10. Asian Cycling Confederation (ACC), Union Europeéne De Cyclisme (European Cycling Union), Oceanian Cycling Confederation; Confederación Panamericana de Ciclismo, Confédération Africaine de Cyclisme.

QUIZ 5: CYCLING TERMS (1)

1. The peloton or bunch; 2. A puncture; 3. The rider who sacrifices his own chances of victory to help his teammate win; 4. A racer's list of achievements, accomplishments or wins; 5. A race held over a specified number of laps on a closed course on public roads closed to traffic; 6. A vehicle that follows the race "sweeping up" abandoned riders; 7. An echelon; 8. The drops; 9. Cadence; 10. Bonk.

QUIZ 6: CYCLING TERMS (2)

1. A slang term for a fixed gear bike; 2. When a cyclist flips over the handlebars, end over end; 3. Local bike shops; 4. Chamois; 5. Panniers; 6. Wheelbase; 7. Slipstream; 8. A manoeuvre where the rider stops the bike and attempts to remain standing; 9. A

Swedish word meaning "speed play," it is a training technique based on unstructured changes in pace and intensity. It can be used instead of timed or measured interval training; 10. A sportive in which, a group of participants attempt to cycle long distances within a pre-defined time limit, at a steady pace set by a road captain. Typically, the group aims to cycle at 22.5 kmph.

QUIZ 7: GRAND TOURS (1)

1. Tour De France, Giro d'Italia, Vuelta a España; 2. The Tour de France; 3. May (Giro), July (Tour) and August (Vuelta); 4. Eddy Merckx, Bernard Hinault and Chris Froome; 5. Seven; 6. Eddy Merckx, Bernard Hinault, Jacques Anquetil, Felice Gimondi, Alberto Contador, Vincenzo Nibali, and Chris Froome; 7. No; 8. Luis Herrera (Col) who won the Vuelta; 9. Five; 10. Djamolidine Abdoujaparov, Mark Cavendish, Laurent Jalabert, Eddy Merckx, and Alessandro Petacchi.

QUIZ 8: GRAND TOURS (2)

1. Six times; 2. Twenty; 3. Erik Zabel; 4. Two; 5. Federico Bahamontes and Luis Herrera; 6. Andy Schleck and Tadej Pogacar (Four wins); 7. Three; 8. Miguel Poblet (1956); Pierino Baffi (1958) and Alessandro Petacchi (2003); 9. Sixty-four; 10. Matteo Tosatto (34 participations, 28 finishes).

QUIZ 9: TOUR DE FRANCE: GENERAL (1)

1. Au Reveil Matin, in Montgeron near Paris; 2. Sixty; 3. The Big Loop; 4. Last place; 5. 1930; 6. Eddy Merckx and Mark Cavendish (34 stage wins each); 7. Richard Virenque; 8. Bordeaux; 9. First rider to reach the highest point of elevation in the race; 10. 1975.

QUIZ 10: TOUR DE FRANCE: GENERAL (2)

1. Jacques Anquetil, Eddy Merckx, Bernard Hinault and Miguel Indurain; 2. Once; 3. Parc Des Princes; 4. The Devil; 5. 1935; 6. He jumped over the Tour on a mountain bike; 7. €500,000; 8. 1939 in Bourg St Maurice; 9. Ten times; 10. His race number consists of a white number on a red background instead of the usual black on white.

QUIZ 11: TOUR DE FRANCE: 1903-1937

1. Maurice Garin (Fra); 2. Fifth, the first four finishers and all stage winners were all disqualified in December 1904; 3. By a points-based system; 4. 1910; 5. Octave Lapize (Fra); 6. Eugene Christophe (Fra); 7. Oldest Tour winner (aged 36 years and 4 months); 8. Évian-Les-Bains; 9. 1924 & 1925; 10. Charles Holland and Bill Burl.

QUIZ 12: TOUR DE FRANCE: 1938-1959

1. Gino Bartali (Ita); 2. François Neuville (Bel); 3. Jean Robic; 4. 1951; 5. Louison Bobet (1953-55); 6. Alpe d'Huez; 7. The Netherlands; 8. Belgium; 9. Charly Gaul (Lux); 10. Federico Bahamontes (Spa).

QUIZ 13: TOUR DE FRANCE: 1960s

1. Roger Rivière (Fra); 2. Belgium; 3. Jan Janssen (Pelforth-Sauvage-Lejeune); 4. 1964; 5. Tom Simpson (GBR); 6. Doping Controls; 7. Five times; 8. Vélodrome De Vincenne; 9. He won the General, Points and King of the Mountains Classifications; 10. Barry Hoban.

QUIZ 14: TOUR DE FRANCE: 1970s

1. Limoges; 2. Luis Ocaña (Bic); 3. Bernard Thévenet (Peugeot-BP-Michelin); 4. Four; 5. Kas-Kaskol; 6. A spectator leapt from the crowd and punched Merckx in the kidney; 7. 2545 miles; 8. Freddy Maertens (Flandria-Velda-Lano); 9. Ti-Raleigh-McGregor; 10. 1975.

QUIZ 15: TOUR DE FRANCE: 1980s

1. Joop Zoetemelk (Ti-Raleigh-Creda); 2. Five; 3. Ángel Arroyo (Spa); 4. Luis Herrera (Varta-Café De Colombia-Mavic); 5. West Berlin; 6. He had been involved in a shooting accident; 7.

Stephen Roche (Carrera-Inoxpran); 8. Eric Breukink (Panasonic-Merckx-Agu); 9. Cauterets; 10. Eight seconds.

QUIZ 16: TOUR DE FRANCE: 1990s

1. 300km. 2. Ariostea; 3. ETA; 4. A policeman taking a photograph; 5. The opening of the Channel Tunnel. 6. Pamplona; 7. Dublin; 8. Cedric Vasseur (Gan); 9. He threw his water bottle at Frenchman, Frederic Moncassin, during a sprint finish; 10. Festina.

QUIZ 17: TOUR DE FRANCE: 2000s

1. Laurent Jalabert (CSC-Tiscali); 2. Joseba Beloki (O.N.C.E.); 3. It was held as a mountain time trial; 4. Thomas Voeckler (Brioches La Boulangère); 5. Alexander Vinokourov (Team Telekom); 6. Óscar Pereiro (Caisse d'Epargne-Illes Baleares); 7. Canterbury; 8. Châteauroux; 9. Carlos Sastre (Team CSC-Saxo Bank); 10. Mont Ventoux.

QUIZ 18: TOUR DE FRANCE: 2010-2020

1. Johnny Hoogerland (Vacansoleil); 2. Cadel Evans (Team BMC); 3. Three; 4. Saxo-Tinkoff; 5. Thibaut Pinot (Française des Jeux); 6. Steve Cummings (MTN-Qhubeka); 7. High winds were forecast at the summit; 8. Fifteen; 9. Dan Martin (UAE Team Emirates). 10. Sam Bennett (Deceuninck-Quickstep).

QUIZ 19: GIRO D'ITALIA (1)

1. 1909; 2. Luigi Ganna (Ita); 3. Cima Coppi; 4. To not participate; 5. 1967; 6. Andy Hampston (USA); 7. Evgeni Berzin (Mecair-Ballan); 8. Forty-two; 9. Gilberto Simoni (Ita); 10. Colle delle Finestre.

QUIZ 20: GIRO D'ITALIA (2)

1. The Mortirolo. 2. The wet roads; 3. Carlos Sastre (Cervélo Test Team); 4. Cadel Evans (Team BMC); 5. Wouter Weylandt (Leopard Trek); 6. One point; 7. Orica GreenEdge; 8. Israel; 9. Three; 10. RCS Sport.

QUIZ 21: VUELTA A ESPAÑA (1)

1. 1935; 2. Red; 3. Roberto Heras (Spa); 4. Chris Horner (41 years and 327 days); 5. Iñigo Cuesta (17 participations); 6. Delio Rodriguez Barros (39 wins); 7. 30.4km (19.2 miles); 8. Blue; 9. 1988; 10. 1998.

QUIZ 22: VUELTA A ESPAÑA (2)

1. Thirty-two; 2. 1999; 3. Laurent Jalabert (O.N.C.E.); 4. He handed in his race number in protest; 5. Assen in the Netherlands; 6. The Basque Country; 7. Pamplona; 8. Caja Rural; 9. Fighting; 10. A burst paddling pool.

QUIZ 23: MILAN SAN REMO (1)

1. 1907; 2. Lucien Petit-Breton (Fra); 3. Passo Del Turchino; 4. Via Roma; 5. A Snowstorm; 6. Luigi Ganna (Ita); 7. Constante Girardengo (Ita); 8. Rudi Altig (Salvarani); 9. Cipressa and Poggio; 10. Tour of Flanders, Paris-Roubaix, Liége-Bastogne-Liége, Tour of Lombardy.

QUIZ 24: MILAN SAN REMO (2)

1. Laurent Fignon (Système U); 2. Le Manie; 3. Erik Zabel (Team Telekom); 4. A millimeter; 5. Gerald Ciolek (MTN-Qhubeka); 6. Pompeiana; 7. Michal Kwiatkowski (Team Sky); 8. August (due to the Covid-19 pandemic); 9. 2005; 10. Zoulfia Zabirova (Rus).

QUIZ 25: TOUR OF FLANDERS (1)

1. 1913; 2. Paul Deman (Automoto-Continental); 3. Rik Van Steenbergen (19 Years and 206 Days); 4. Andrei Tchmil (37 years and 71 days; 5. Twice; 6. Bruges; 7. 12.9%; 8. 25%; 9. A Chapel; 10. Tenbosse, Muur de Geraardsbergen, and the Bosberg.

QUIZ 26: TOUR OF FLANDERS (2)

1. Fiorenzo Magni (Wilier Triestina); 2. Tom Simpson (Rapha-Gitane-Dunlop); 3. Jan Raas (Ti-Raleigh-McGregor); 4. Johan Museeuw (Mapei). 5. Gianluca Bortalami (Vini Caldirola); 6.

Stijn Devolder (Quick-step); 7. Antwerp; 8. Adri and Mathieu van der Poel; 9. Tom Boonen and Fabian Cancellara. 10. Louison Bobet (1955), Rik Van Looy (1962); Eddy Merckx (1975); Tom Boonen (2006) and Peter Sagan (2016).

QUIZ 27: PARIS ROUBAIX (1)

1. 1896; 2. Josef Fischer (Ger); 3. 1000 Francs; 4. Theodore Vienne and Maurice Perez; 5. Gilbert Duclos-Lassalle (38 years and 8 months in 1993); 6. Belgium (57 wins); 7. Roger De Vlaeminck & Tom Boonen (4 wins each); 8. Compiegne; 9. A mounted cobblestone; 10. Roubaix Velodrome.

QUIZ 28: PARIS ROUBAIX (2)

1. Troisvilles; 2. Arenberg; 3. Carrefour de l'Arbre; 4. Charles Crupelandt; 5. Felice Gimondi (Salvarani); 6. Sean Kelly; 7. Team Mapei-GB; 8; Stuart O'Grady (Team CSC); 9. Michael Goolaerts (Vérandas Willems-Crelan); 10. The 2 World Wars and the Covid-19 pandemic.

QUIZ 29: LIÈGE-BASTOGNE-LIÈGE (1)

1. 1892; 2. L'Express; 3. 17; 4. He had changed bikes; 5. Spa; 6. Eddy Merckx (5 wins); 7. Snowfall; 8. Germain Derijcke was first over the finish line, but he had crossed a closed level crossing. He had a 3-minute lead over Frans Schoubben in second place and officials deemed he had not gained that much

time from the illegal railway crossing; 9. Seven; 10. Ferdinand Kübler (1951 & 1952), Stan Ockers (1955), Eddy Merckx (1972); Moreno Argentin (1991); Davide Rebellin (2004); Alejandro Valverde (2006, 2015 & 2017), Philippe Gilbert (2011).

QUIZ 30: LIÈGE-BASTOGNE-LIÈGE (2)

1. 12.5%; 2. 4.4km or 2.2miles; 3. The Côte de Saint-Nicolas; 4. Tyler Hamilton (Team CSC); 5. Simon Gerrans (Orica GreenEdge); 6. He had paid his breakaway companion, Alexander Kolobnev, €100,000 to not contest the final sprint; 7. He had won all 4 'hilly' classics in 10 days (Brabantse Pijl, Amstel Gold Race, Flèche Wallonne and Liège); 8. A 600-metre stretch of cobbles on the Côte de la Rue Naniot; 9. 2017; 10. Annemiek Van Vleuten (Mitchelton-Scott).

QUIZ 31: TOUR OF LOMBARDY (1)

1. 1905; 2. Giovanni Gerbi (Ita); 3. October; 4. The Classic of the Falling (Dead) Leaves; 5. Lake Como; 6. Bergamo; 7. Mendrisio; 8. Lecco; 9. Muro di Sormano; 10. Madonna del Ghisallo.

QUIZ 32: TOUR OF LOMBARDY (2)

1. Gino Bartali (Ita); 2. Tom Simpson (Peugeot-BP-Michelin); 3. Oscar Camenzind (Mapei-Bricobi); 4. 2004, 2007 and 2008; 5. Paolo Bettini (Quick-Step-Davitamon); 6. Oliver Zaugg (Leopard Trek); 7. Fausto Coppi (5 wins); 8. Henri Pelissier and

Sean Kelly; 9. 21; 10. Fausto Coppi (1949) and Eddy Merckx (1972).

QUIZ 33: THE UCI WORLD TOUR (1)

1. The Tour Down Under; 2. Siena; 3. Omloop Het Nieuwsblad; 4. 1933; 5. Greg Van Avermaet (CCC Pro Team); 6. The Mur de Huy; 7. A basque beret; 8. 2005. 9. The Kemmelberg; 10. Simon Yates (Mitchelton-Scott).

QUIZ 34: THE UCI WORLD TOUR (2)

1. Sean Kelly (7 wins); 2. Krakow; 3. Dan Martin (Garmin-Sharp); 4. Peter Kennaugh (Team Sky); 5. It is held over just two days; 6. Plouay; 7. Andrei Kivilev (Cofidis); 8. Cadel Evans; 9. The UAE Tour; 10. Simon Gerrans (4 wins).

QUIZ 35: OTHER UCI TOUR RACES (1)

1. The Tour of Oman; 2. Tom Boonen (Quick-Step-Davitamon); 3. 1896; 4. It is usually held over a 5- or 6-day period; 5. Lars Petter Nordhaug (Team Sky); 6. China; 7. Oscar Freire (Rabobank); 8. The Tour de Langkawi; 9. Bauke Mollema (Trek-Segafredo); 10. A horse.

QUIZ 36: OTHER UCI TOUR RACES (2)

1. Tony Martin (Ger); 2. A train; 3. Tom Danielson (Mercury Cycling Team); 4. Giro del Trentino; 5. Winner Anacona (Movistar); 6. Two days; 7. 2016; 8. Scheldeprijs; 9. Thor Hushovd; 10. He crashed on the final bend with 1km to go, picked himself up, replaced his chain which had come loose and crossed the finish line inches ahead of sprint king, Marcel Kittel.

QUIZ 37: THE WORLD CHAMPIONSHIPS (1)

1. Denmark (in 1921); 2. Alfredo Binda (Ita); 3. The Rainbow Jersey; 4. Italy (with 144); 5. Nine (5 Road & 4 ITT); 6. Greg Lemond (in 1989); 7. 2009; 8. The World Championship Road Race and two of the three Grand Tours; 9. Two; 10. Eddy Merckx and Stephen Roche.

QUIZ 38: THE WORLD CHAMPIONSHIPS (2)

1. Chris Boardman (GBR); 2. Laurent Brochard (Festina); 3. Michael Rogers (Quickstep-Davitamon); 4. Copenhagen; 4. BMC Team Racing. 5. Richmond, USA (2015), Doha, Qatar (2016) and Bergen, Norway (2017); 7. Mount Fløyen; 8. 1958; 9. Beryl Burton (GBR); 10. Rwanda.

QUIZ 39: THE OLYMPICS (1)

1. Annemiek Van Vleuten; 2. Lotus; 3. 2008 Beijing Olympics; 4. Great Britain; 5. 1996 Atlanta Olympics; 6. Alexander

Vinokourov (Kaz); 7. Bart Brentjens; 8. Fabio Casartelli (Ita); 9. Helen Constance Carpenter-Phinney; 10. Max Sciandri.

QUIZ 40: THE OLYMPICS (2)

1. Vyacheslav Ekimov (Rus); 2. Seventeen; 3. Miguel Indurain (Spa); 4. 1964 Tokyo Olympics; 5. The Team Pursuit; 6. Mariana Pajón (Col); 7. Germany; 8. Rowing; 9. Kristin Armstrong (USA); 10. Aristidis Konstantinidis (Gre).

QUIZ 41: BRITISH CYCLING (1)

1. Sir Bradley Wiggins; 2. Graeme Obree; 3. Steve Joughin; 4. Robert Millar or Phillipa York; 5. Geraint Thomas; 6. Marcin Bialoblocki; 7. The Snaefell Mountain Course (Isle of Man TT); 8. David Millar; 9. Michael Hutchinson; 10. Andy Wilkinson, who completed the journey in 41 hours, 4 minutes, and 22 seconds on a Windcheetah Recumbent Tricycle.

QUIZ 42: BRITISH CYCLING (2)

1. Three; 2. Sir Chris Hoy; 3. Mark Cavendish; 4. Ghent in Belgium; 5. Sir Dave Brailsford; 6. 1945; 7. Twice; 8. Steve Cummings (Team Dimension Data); 9. Hugh Carthy (Cannondale-Drapac); 10. Tom Simpson (1965), Sir Chris Hoy (2008), Mark Cavendish (2011), Sir Bradley Wiggins (2012), Geraint Thomas (2018).

QUIZ 43: WOMEN'S CYCLING (1)

1. Lizzie Armistead in 2012; 2. Arlenis Sierra (Astana); 3. Twice; 4. Megan Guarnier (Boels-Dolmans); 5. 1988; 6. Nicole Cooke (Raleigh-Lifeforce-Creation HB Pro Cycling Team); 7. Fabiana Luperini in 1998; 8. Anna Van Der Breggen and Annemiek Van Vleuten (2 wins each); 9. Marie Purvis; 10. Emma Pooley (Cervelo Test Team).

QUIZ 44: WOMEN'S CYCLING (2)

1. Ellen Van Dijk (Hol); 2. Hanka Kupfernagel (Ger); 3. Three times (in 2006, 2012 and 2013); 4. Sara Ballantyne (USA); 5. The Prudential RideLondon Classique (with a 1st prize of £91,500); 6. Katie Hall (Team United Healthcare); 7. Fifth; 8. Katarzyna Niewiadoma (WM3 Pro Cycling); 9. Jeannie Longo (Fra); 10. The leader, Swiss cyclist Nicole Hanselmann, caught up to the men's race which had started 10 minutes before the women's race.

QUIZ 45: TRACK CYCLING (1)

1. Braking system; 2. Derny; 3. Schuermann Architects; 4. 250m (820ft); 5. 200 metres to go; 6. The Forest City Velodrome in London, Ontario, Canada at 138m (453ft); 7. Preston Park Velodrome in Brighton, UK (built in 1877); 8. Parc des Princes; 9. New Zealand; 10. Scratch Race, Tempo Race, Elimination Race, and Points Race.

QUIZ 46: TRACK CYCLING (2)

1. Miguel Indurain; 2. Luís Carlos Galán velodrome in Bogota, Colombia; 3. 1993; 4. The Six Days of Ghent; 5. The Scratch Race; 6. Three; 7. Grégory Baugé (Fra); 8. Sprint Time Trial, Flying Lap, and Individual Pursuit; 9. Kristina Vogel; 10. Germany (10 wins).

QUIZ 47: CYCLO-CROSS (1)

1. 1924; 2. Paris; 3. 1950; 4. The Bunnyhop; 5. Slovakia; 6. Pauline Ferrand-Prévot (Fra); 7. 1987; 8. Eli Iserbyt (Bel); 9. Yorkshire; 10. Portland, Oregon.

QUIZ 48: CYCLO-CROSS (2)

1. Eight rounds; 2. Sven Nys (13 wins); 3. 2015; 4. All of them. 5. Four times; 6. 1993; 7. Las Vegas; 8. Tom Pidcock (GBR); 9. Zdeněk Štybar (Cze); 10. 2009.

QUIZ 49: MOUNTAIN BIKING (1)

1. Joe Breeze; 2. 1990; 3. Julien Absalon (Fra); 4. Steve Peat (GBR); 5. Guy Martin; 6. Four times; 7. Michael Rasmussen (Den); 8. Catherine Prendel (Can); 9. Fort William, UK; 10. Reece Wilson (GBR).

QUIZ 50: MOUNTAIN BIKING (2)

1. South Africa; 2. 1989; 3. Anne Caroline Chausson (Fra); 4. Tracy Moseley; 5. Brian Skinner; 6. Scott-SRAM MTB Racing Team; 7. Aaron Gwin (USA); 8. Rachel Atherton; 9. Twenty-Four Hours; 10. Canyon.

QUIZ 51: BMX (1)

1. 1982 (first official ones in 1993); 2. 2008; 3. BMX Freestyle; 4. Baku, Azerbaijan; 5. 1977; 6. Ipswich; 7. 1981; 8. Māris Ŝtrombergs (Lat); 9. Part of a BMX course where the landing point is at a higher elevation than the take-off point; 10. David Duffield.

QUIZ 52: BMX (2)

1. Palms Park in West Los Angeles; 2. Schwinn Stingray; 3. 1974; 4. Dale Holmes (GBR); 5. Caroline Buchanan (Aus); 6. USA + France; 7. 2009; 8. 2010; 9. Liam Phillips (GBR); 10. Laura Smulders (Ned).

QUIZ 53: GRAN FONDO / CYCLOSPORTIVE (1)

1. 2011; 2. Tour of Flanders Cyclosportive; 3. Wedgwood; 4. Sabiñánigo; 5. 1993; 6. Christophe Rinero; 7. La Marmotte; 8. New Zealand; 9. Riders must ride vintage bikes (pre-1987) and wear vintage clothing; 10. Gran Fondo Australia, Gran Fondo

Coimbra Region, Gran Fondo Antalya, Gran Fondo Vosges, Tour Lakeland, Gran Fondo Isle of Man.

QUIZ 54: GRAN FONDO / CYCLOSPORTIVE (2)

1. Levi Leipheimer; 2. Marzio Bruseghin; 3. Col de la Colombière, Col des Aravis and Col des Saisies; 4. Shay Elliot, who was Ireland's first ever wearer of the Yellow Jersey; 5. 1970; 6. Six; 7. Bordeaux-Paris; 8. 16000; 9. Alpe d'Huez; 10. Varese, Italy.

QUIZ 55: TRIATHLON (1)

1. Swimming; cycling and running; 2. International Triathlon Union; 3. 1989; 4. 12 miles (20km); 5. 2000; 6. A time penalty; 7. 2009; 8. Javier Gomez (Spa); 9. Alistair and Jonathan Brownlee; 10. Mario Mola (Spa).

QUIZ 56: TRIATHLON (2)

1. New Zealand; 2. Katie Zaferes (USA); 3. 1991; 4. Hamish Carter (NZ); 5. Annabel Luxford (Aus); 6. Marble Arch, London to Arc de Triomphe, Paris; 7. World Triathlon Corporation; 8. Kailua-Kona, Hawaii; 9. 112 miles (180.25km); 10. Lionel Sanders (Can).

QUIZ 57: SPONSORS (1)

1. Hair care products; 2. 1998; 3. Banking; 4. Chemical products for the building industry; 5. Segafredo; 6. A French jewelry retailer; 7. Life insurance and pension management; 8. An anti-abortion, anti-euthanasia group backed by the Catholic Church; 9. Belisol; 10. Blanco.

QUIZ 58: SPONSORS (2)

1. Plant food; 2. Domina Vacanze; 3. Making expresso machines; 4. France's national lottery; 5. Brandy; 6. GreenEdge; 7. Supermarkets; 8. Cold meats (salami); 9. The National Organization of Spanish Blind People; 10. A children's clothing manufacturer.

QUIZ 59: BRANDS (1)

1. Altura; 2. Kask; 3. GT; 4. Etxe Ondo; 5. Oakley; 6. Science-In-Sport; 7. Endura; 8. Santini; 9. Cannondale; 10. Fizik.

QUIZ 60: BRANDS (2)

1. 1876; 2. Sidi; 3. Paceline; 4. Cleaning Products (lubes, degreasers etc); 5. 1840; 6. Look; 7. Pinarello; 8. Doping for the Hair; 9. Nalini. 10. 1933.

QUIZ 61: NICKNAMES (1)

1. Miguel Indurain; 2. Marco Pantani; 3. Federico Bahamontes; 4. Eddy Merckx; 5. Peter Sagan; 6. Fabian Cancellara; 7. Mario Cipollini; 8. Johan Museeuw; 9. Alberto Contador; 10. Bernard Hinault.

QUIZ 62: NICKNAMES (2)

1. Mark Cavendish; 2. Robbie McEwen; 3. Fausto Coppi; 4. Greg Lemond; 5. Chris Boardman (or Laurent Fignon); 6. Jan Ullrich; 7. Geraint Thomas; 8. Paolo Bettini; 9. Andrea Tafi; 10. Pedro Delgado.

QUIZ 63: CYCLING RECORDS (1)

1. Denise Mueller-Korenek; 2. Éric Barone; 3. Victor Campenaerts (Bel); 4. 56.375km (35.03 miles); 5. Francesco Russo (Swi); 6. 568.8 miles (915.39km); 7. Christine MacKenzie; 8. 55 hours and 59 minutes; 9. 19; 10. Alberto Contador (4 wins).

QUIZ 64: CYCLING RECORDS (2)

1. Paolo Bettini (3); 2. 11 hours; 3. Mark Beaumont; 4. Filippo Ganna (Ita); 5. Kristina Vogel (Ger); 6. Christoph Strasser; 7. 13.23mph; 8. He cycled 6708m under water; 9. Eleven; 10. Zwift.

QUIZ 65: KING OF THE MOUNTAINS (1)

1. Alto de Jaizkibel; 2. Mount Baldy; 3. Twenty-one; 4. Tour of Britain; 5. Isle of Man; 6. Alto de l'Angliru at 24%; 7. Alberto Contador (Spa); 8. Italy; 9. Col De La Bonette-Restefond, at 2802 metres; 10. France and Spain.

QUIZ 66: KING OF THE MOUNTAINS (2)

1. 15.3km or 9.5miles; 2. Vuelta a Burgos; 3. Amstel Gold Race; 4. Grossglockner; 5. Igor Anton (Euskaltel); 6. After crashing he was unable to get a replacement bike and ran up it until he could; 7. 12.1% at the summit (from the south side); 8. 1750 metres; 9. Tour of the Basque Country; 10. Le Bourg-d'Oisans.

QUIZ 67: GEOGRAPHY (1)

1. Denver, Colorado; 2. GP Cycliste de Montreal and Quebec; 3. Northern Ireland, UK; 4. South Australia; 5. Oudenaarde; 6. Avenue de Grammont; 7. South Africa; 8. Denmark; 9. Geelong; 10. Clasica de San Sebastian.

QUIZ 68: GEOGRAPHY (2)

1. Mallorca; 2. Costa Rica; 3. The Arctic Race of Norway; 4. Spain; 5. Toulouse; 6. Tenerife; 7. Glasgow; 8. Silver City, New Mexico; 9. A church containing a cycling museum; 10. Cassel.

QUIZ 69: LANDMARKS (1)

1. Louvre; 2. 2004; 3. Adelaide Oval; 4. Tour of Poland; 5. Cuenca; 6. Tour of Catalunya; 7. The Guggenheim; 8. Its amphitheatre; 9. Assisi; 10. The Great Wall of China.

QUIZ 70: LANDMARKS (2)

1. Circuito de Getxo; 2. Vienna, Austria; 3. Slovenia; 4. Grand Prix de Wallonie; 5. Eiffel Tower; 6. Easter Island; 7. Malta; 8. 2016; 9. Istanbul; 10. Quebrantahuesos.

QUIZ 71: FOOD AND DRINK (1)

1. The south (particularly around Toulouse and Carcassonne); 2. Powerbar; 3. Musette; 4. His own weight in cheese; 5. Sport in Science; 6. Kas; 7. Kendal; 8. Rioja; 9. Mule Bar; 10. Beer.

QUIZ 72: FOOD AND DRINK (2)

1. Dry pork sausage; 2. Jelly Belly; 3. Somerset; 4. A few kilograms of bananas; 5. Berlin; 6. Wine; 7. Around 6071 calories; 8. Beetroot juice; 9. It came from eating contaminated Spanish beef. 10. Bruges.

QUIZ 73: LITERATURE (1)

1. Mark Twain; 2. Michael Hutchinson; 3. Jane Eastoe; 4. Tour of the Basque Country; 5. Carlton Kirby; 6. French Revolutions; 7. David Millar; 8. H.G. Wells; 9. Matt Seaton; 10. Émile Zola.

QUIZ 74: LITERATURE (2)

1. Tour de France; 2. Nancy Drew; 3. Green; 4. Sherlock Holmes; 5. Albert Einstein; 6. Tim Krabbé; 7. William Fotheringham; 8. Sir Arthur Conan Doyle; 9. How I Won the Yellow Jumper; 10. John F. Kennedy.

QUIZ 75: AT THE MOVIES (1)

1. Kuwahara; 2. Graeme Obree; 3. Team CSC; 4. Bicycle Thieves; 5. Ben Foster; 6. A Sunday in Hell; 7. Nicole Kidman; 8. Team HTC-Columbia; 9. Belleville Rendezvous (also known as 'Les Triplets de Bellville'); 10. Kevin Costner.

QUIZ 76: AT THE MOVIES (2)

1. The Ho Chi Minh Trail; 2. Kevin Bacon; 3. The Trans Am Bike Race; 4. Jennifer Grey; 5. Tim Burton; 6. Uluru (Ayers Rock); 7. Dennis Quaid; 8. Eric Idle; 9. Premium Rush; 10. David Millar.

QUIZ 77: TELEVISION (1)

1. 1948; 2. Tour Down Under; 3. David Duffield; 4. Larry & George Lamb; 5. Phil Liggett; 6. It was deemed to create a 'climate of fear' about cars; 7. 2017; 8. A bicycle-powered television; 9. TVE; 10. Sean Kelly.

QUIZ 78: TELEVISION (2)

1. Open All Hours; 2. Stranger Things; 3. Matt Barbet; 4. France Televisions and Euro Media France; 5. Brian Smith; 6. Alaska and Patagonia; 7. Paul Sherwen; 8. Clare Balding; 9. 112.94mph (181.76kmh); 10. Sir Bradley Wiggins.

QUIZ 79: THE MUSIC ROUND (1)

1. Mark Ronson and the Business INTL; 2. Shakira; 3. 1978; 4. Kraftwerk; 5. Natalie Imbruglia; 6. Sheryl Crow; 7. Nine Million; 8. The Vuelta; 9. Sia; 10. Orica GreenEdge.

QUIZ 80: THE MUSIC ROUND (2)

1. White; 2. Tom Waits; 3. The Mixtures; 4. Pink Floyd; 5. A Head Full of Dreams; 6. Danny MacAskill; 7. David Byrne; 8. The Chemical Brothers; 9. 2500 miles (4000km); 10. "Bicycle, Bicycle, Bicycle, I want to ride my bicycle."

ABOUT THE AUTHOR

Philip Carter is a cycling enthusiast and has travelled all over the World to watch bike races. As a proud Manxman he was privileged to be in France in 2011 and 2016 to see Mark Cavendish wearing the Green and Yellow Jerseys. He counts the Tour Down Under as the best stage race, for accessibility to the riders and stages, the weather and of course the wine. He has ridden cyclosportives in Flanders and the UK and cycled up the odd Pyrenean mountain. Aside from cycling, Manchester United is his other passion and he tries to attend a couple of matches each season.

Printed in Great Britain
by Amazon

13495528R00068